T0201693

# Diving
# Dolphin

**FIRST EDITION**
**Series Editor** Deborah Lock; **Project Editor** Caryn Jenner; **Art Editors** Jane Horne, Rashika Kachroo;
**US Editors** Regina Kahney, Shannon Beatty; **Managing Editor** Soma Chowdhury;
**Managing Art Editor** Ahlawat Gunjan; **Production Editor** Marc Staples; **DTP Designer** Anita Yadav;
**Picture Researchers** Angela Anderson, Sumedha Chopra;
**Jacket Designers** Natalie Godwin, Martin Wilson; **Publishing Manager** Bridget Giles;
**Art Director** Martin Wilson; **Natural History Consultant** Theresa Greenaway;
**Reading Consultant** Linda Gambrell, PhD

**THIS EDITION**
**Editorial Management** by Oriel Square
**Produced for DK** by WonderLab Group LLC
Jennifer Emmett, Erica Green, Kate Hale, *Founders*

**Editors** Grace Hill Smith, Libby Romero, Michaela Weglinski;
**Photography Editors** Kelley Miller, Annette Kiesow, Nicole DiMella; **Managing Editor** Rachel
Houghton; **Designers** Project Design Company; **Researcher** Michelle Harris; **Copy Editor** Lori Merritt;
**Indexer** Connie Binder; **Proofreader** Larry Shea; **Reading Specialist** Dr. Jennifer L. Albro;
**Curriculum Specialist** Elaine Larson

**Published in the United States by DK Publishing**
1745 Broadway, 20th Floor, New York, NY 10019

Copyright © 2023 Dorling Kindersley Limited
DK, a Division of Penguin Random House LLC
23 24 25 26 10 9 8 7 6 5 4 3 2 1
001-334009-July/2023

A catalog record for this book
is available from the Library of Congress.
HC ISBN: 978-0-7440-7342-3
PB ISBN: 978-0-7440-7343-0

DK books are available at special discounts when purchased in bulk for sales promotions, premiums,
fundraising, or educational use. For details, contact: DK Publishing Special Markets,
1745 Broadway, 20th Floor, New York, NY 10019
SpecialSales@dk.com

Printed and bound in China

The publisher would like to thank the following for their kind permission to reproduce their images:
a=above; c=center; b=below; l=left; r=right; t=top; b/g=background

**Alamy Stock Photo:** Brandon Cole Marine Photography 14br, imageBROKER / Norbert Probst 26-27t,
Natalia Pryanishnikova 7cb, Steve Bloom Images / Steve Bloom 20-21t, Karen van der Zijden 15;
**Dreamstime.com:** Dejan / alenka Sarman / hren 12-13b, Ig0rzh 19, Izanbar 9cr, 30tl, Shawn Jackson 30clb,
Daisuke Kurashima 30bl, Graeme Snow 30cla; **Getty Images:** Corbis Documentary / Stuart Westmorland 8,
Image Source / Stephen Frink 18cl, Moment / Brent Durand 16-17b; **Getty Images / iStock:** Nicolas Sanchez-Biezma
28-29b, Rainer von Brandis 9cla, Serge Melesan 22tl, slowmotiongli 26tl; naturepl.com: Tony Wu 24-25b;
**Science Photo Library:** Clay Coleman 6-7t; **Shutterstock.com:** slowmotiongli 10-11t

Cover images: *Front:* **Shutterstock.com:** AnnstasAg, YG Studio c; *Back:* **Shutterstock.com:** NBvector clb,
Pacha M Vector ca, YG Studio cra

All other images © Dorling Kindersley
For more information see: www.dkimages.com

## For the curious
**www.dk.com**

# Diving
# Dolphin

Karen Wallace

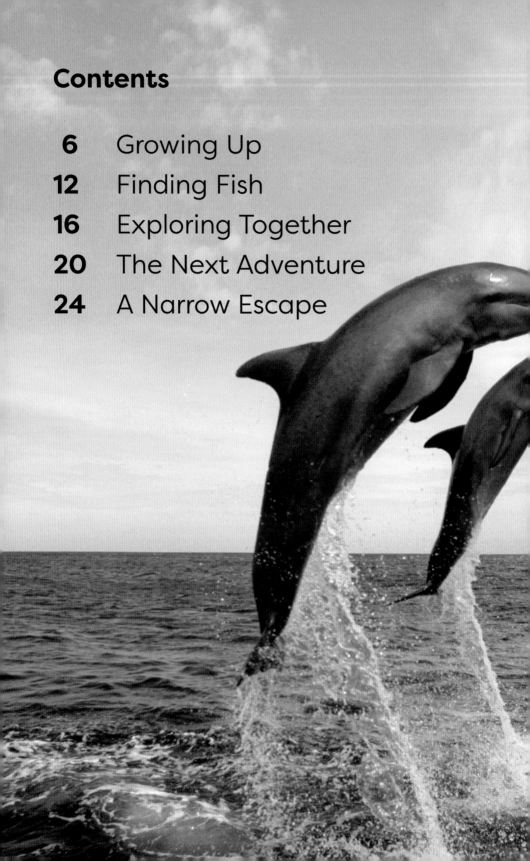

# Contents

## Growing Up

A young dolphin dives
through the water.
Its shiny skin is as
smooth as satin.
Far below, it sees
its mother.

Its mother is swimming
with her new baby.

**blowhole**

The young dolphin leaps. It breathes in air through a blowhole on the top of its head.

The dolphin dives again.
A turtle watches it.

An octopus waggles past
through the water.

Then, the young dolphin
swims away with older
dolphins.
It leaves its mother and
the new baby behind.

It twirls and leaps with
the older dolphins.
They splash the water
with their tails.

# Finding Fish

Hundreds of fish flash through the water. The fish turn together.

The dolphins follow.
The frightened fish swim
around in circles.

The dolphins snatch
the fish.
Their teeth are sharp.
They gulp the fish
down whole.

The young dolphin
is growing.
It is always hungry.
It eats
and eats
to fill
its belly.

# Exploring Together

The dolphins move on.
They turn and dive.
They spin and tumble.

They squeal and whistle.
When one swims off,
the others follow.

The young dolphin roams the ocean.
It hunts for fish through beds of seaweed.

seaweed

It rides the fast waves.
The waves push it over the sparkling water.

19

## The Next Adventure

The sun is setting.
The dolphin leaps in the
smooth sea.
The fish are hiding.

The dolphin sees
the silver fish in
the water.
They glow like stars
far below.

orca

The dolphin chases
the fish.
It swims down and down
to the sandy seabed.

The dolphin does not know that orcas are watching it from above. The orcas are hungry.

# A Narrow Escape

The orcas shoot
through the water.
Their jaws are strong.
Their teeth are
like knives.

The young dolphin gives a warning whistle. It races away with the other dolphins.

The orcas swim through
the water.
The dolphins hear them
coming closer.

The young dolphin hides.
It makes no sound.
This time the orcas
don't find it.

# Home Again

Now, the young dolphin
swims back to its mother.
The baby dolphin
is still with her.
Their flippers touch.

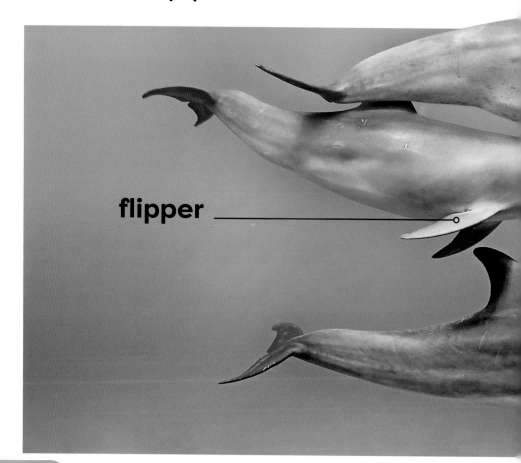

flipper

They rub each other's beaks.
Soon, the dolphin will hunt for fish again.

beak

# Glossary

**beak**
a dolphin's mouth part used for grabbing food

**blowhole**
a hole on a dolphin's head used for breathing in and out

**flipper**
a front limb of a dolphin used for steering as it swims

**orca**
a black and white toothed whale

**seaweed**
a plant that grows in the sea

# Index

# Quiz

Answer the questions to see what you have learned. Check your answers with an adult.

1. Where do dolphins live?

2. What do dolphins eat?

3. What ocean animal eats dolphins?

4. What do dolphins do to warn each other of danger?

5. What are three ways dolphins move in the water?

1. In the ocean  2. Fish  3. Orca  4. Whistle
5. Possible answers: They swim, leap, dive,
twirl, splash, spin, tumble, roam, and ride waves